Farms

Written by Sandra Iversen • Illustrated by Marjory Gardner

This is a farm.
This farmer grows vegetables.
He grows potatoes and carrots.
His farm is called
a vegetable farm.

This is a farm.
This farmer grows crops.
She grows wheat
and other grains.
Her farm is called
a wheat farm.

This is a farm.
This farmer grows fruit.
He grows apples
and plums and peaches.
His farm is called
an orchard.

5

This is a farm.
This farmer keeps cows.
She milks the cows
every morning and every night.
Her farm is called
a dairy farm.

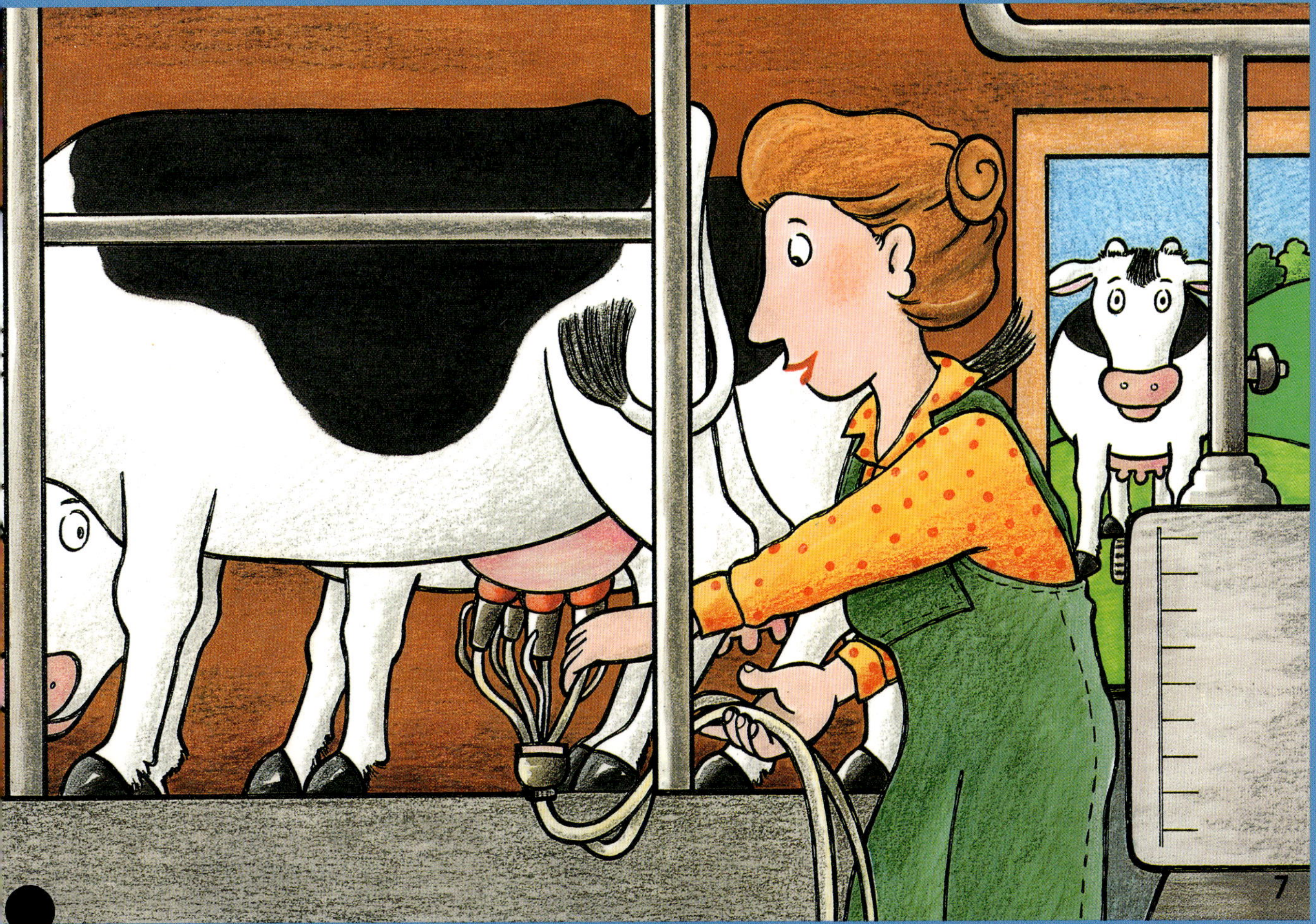

This is a farm.
This farmer raises sheep.
He raises them
for their wool and their meat.
His farm is called
a sheep ranch.

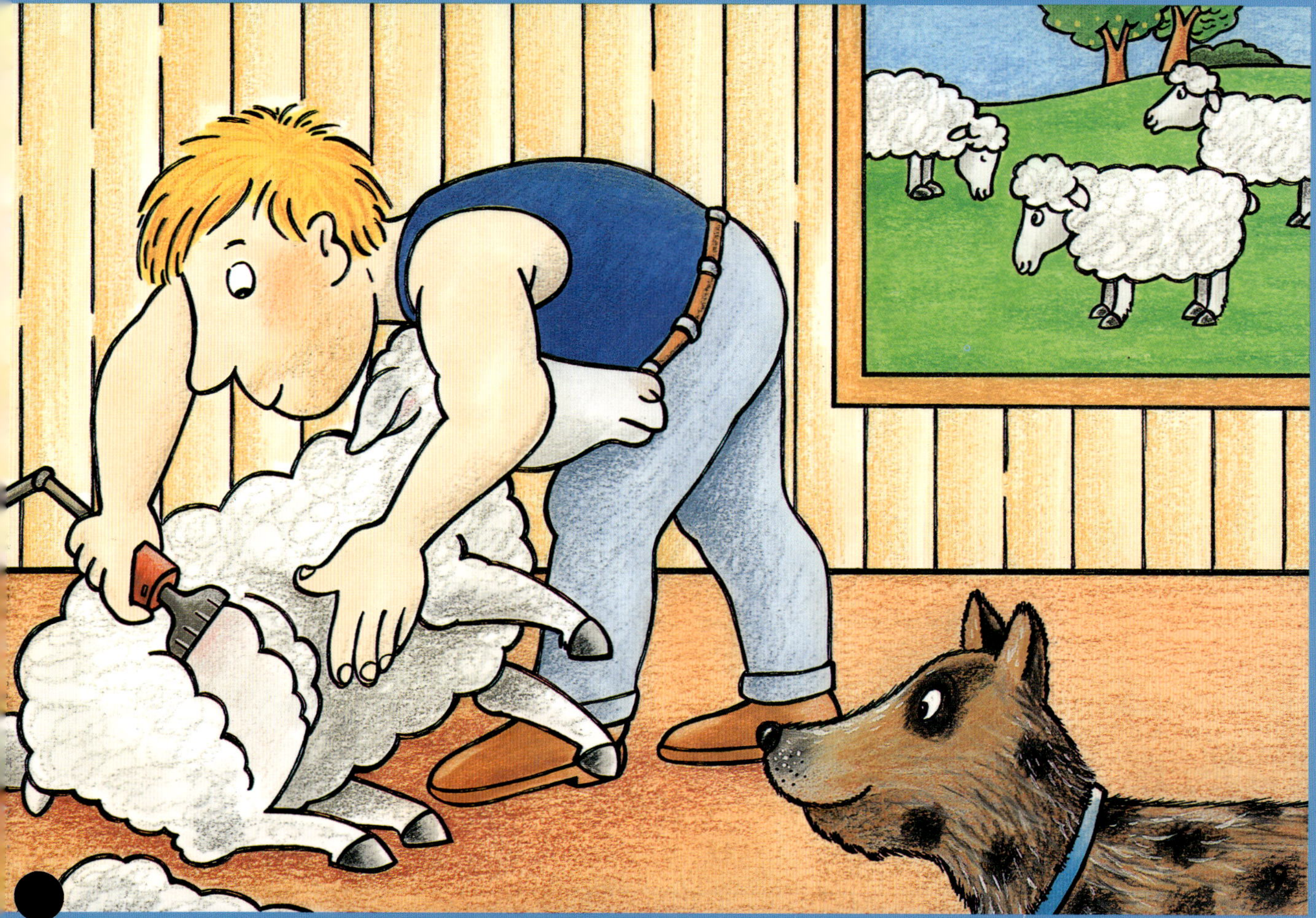

This is a farm.
This farmer farms shellfish.
She grows mussels under the water.
Her farm is called a mussel farm.

11

This is a farm.
This farmer raises cattle.
He raises them for their meat.
His farm is called
a cattle ranch.